MATT

THE SALVATION OF
DOCTOR WHO

LEADER GUIDE
WRITTEN BY JOSH TINLEY

Abingdon Press / Nashville

THE SALVATION OF DOCTOR WHO
LEADER GUIDE

A SMALL GROUP STUDY
CONNECTING CHRIST AND CULTURE

This book is printed on elemental, chlorine-free paper.
ISBN 978-1-5018-0382-6

15 16 17 18 19 20 21 22 23—10 9 8 7 6 5 4 3 2 1
MANUFACTURED IN THE UNITED STATES OF AMERICA

CONTENTS

To the Leader 5

1. The Oldest Question in the Universe. 11

2. God and Time and God's Time 24

3. The Sonic Screwdriver Is Mightier than the Sword . . . 35

4. Bigger on the Inside 49

Note 64

TO THE LEADER

This Pop in Culture Bible study series is a collection of studies about faith and popular culture. Each study uses a work of pop culture as a way to examine questions and issues of the Christian faith. Studies consist of a book, DVD, and leader guide. Our hope and prayer is that the studies will open our eyes to the spiritual truths that exist all around us in books, movies, music, and television.

As we walk with Christ, we discover the divine all around us, and in turn, the world invites us into a deeper picture of its Creator. Through this lens of God's redemption story, we are invited to look at culture in a new and inviting way. We are invited to dive into the realms of literature, art, and entertainment to explore and discover how God is working in and through us and in the world around us to tell his great story of redemption.

In many ways the long-running British science fiction adventure *Doctor Who* is also a story of redemption and hope. For more than fifty years, viewers on both sides of the Atlantic have tuned in to join the mysterious Time Lord known only as "the

Doctor" on his travels through space and time. *Doctor Who* fans have been along for the ride, following the Doctor as he journeys to the farthest reaches of the universe, encounters all manner of life forms, and travels into the distant past and future. In his study *The Salvation of Doctor Who,* author and pastor Matt Rawle explores this British sci-fi classic and invites us to consider this series as a lens through which we can better understand our identities as followers of Christ, discover ways in which God enters our time lines, examine how we can redeem and transform the evil in our midst, and begin to more fully appreciate the wonder and mystery of God.

In this study, we will look at four key aspects of the Doctor's story: his identity; his relationship with time; his adversaries; and his time-traveling vehicle, the TARDIS. We will consider what each can teach us about ourselves and our relationships with God.

HOW TO FACILITATE THIS STUDY

Participants in this study do not need to have seen an episode of *Doctor Who.* They don't need to understand why the TARDIS is larger on the inside than it appears to be from the outside. And they don't need to know what a Dalek looks like. That said, your group will likely get more out of this study if participants have some familiarity with the series. If possible, get together before beginning the study to watch the episode "The Eleventh Hour," the first episode of *Doctor Who's* fifth season. The study book contains a quick refresher of the show in the introductory material, and descriptions of key characters and summaries of particular episodes pop up throughout the book. It is also important that participants take time before each session to read the corresponding chapter in *The Salvation of Doctor Who* and reflect on its questions.

This four-session study makes use of the following components:

- the study book, *The Salvation of Doctor Who* by Matt Rawle
- this Leader Guide
- *The Salvation of Doctor Who* DVD

You will need a DVD player or computer, and a television or projection screen so that you can watch the DVD segments as part of your group session. Participants in the study will also need access to Bibles during the session; many activities will also require basic supplies including a markerboard or large sheets of paper and markers, pens and pencils, and index cards and/or slips of paper.

Each session is structured into a 60-minute format:

- Opening activity and prayer (10 minutes)
- Watch DVD segment (10 minutes)
- Study and discussion (30–35 minutes)
- Closing activity and prayer (5 minutes)

If you have more time in your session, or want to utilize more activities during your session, "Additional Options for Bible Study and Discussion" are included for each chapter, listed after the closing prayer.

Helpful Hints

Preparing for Each Session

- Pray for wisdom and discernment from the Holy Spirit, for you and for each member of the group, as you prepare for the study.
- Before each session, familiarize yourself with the content. Read the study book chapter again.
- Choose the session elements you will use during the group session, including the specific discussion questions you plan to cover. Be prepared, however, to adjust the session as group members interact and as questions arise. Prepare carefully, but allow space for the Holy Spirit to move in and through the group members and through you as facilitator.
- Prepare the space where the group will meet so that the space will enhance the learning process. Ideally, group members should be seated around a table or in a circle so that all can see one another. Movable chairs are best so that the group easily can form pairs or small groups for discussion.

Shaping the Learning Environment

- Create a climate of openness, encouraging group members to participate as they feel comfortable.
- Remember that some people will jump right in with answers and comments, while others need time to process what is being discussed.
- If you notice that some group members seem never to be able to enter the conversation, ask them if they have

thoughts to share. Give everyone a chance to talk, but keep the conversation moving. Moderate to prevent a few individuals from doing all the talking.

- Communicate the importance of group discussions and group exercises.

- If no one answers at first during discussions, do not be afraid of silence. Count silently to ten, then say something such as, "Would anyone like to go first?" If no one responds, venture an answer yourself and ask for comments.

- Model openness as you share with the group. Group members will follow your example. If you limit your sharing to a surface level, others will follow suit.

- Encourage multiple answers or responses before moving on to the next question.

- Ask, "Why?" or "Why do you believe that?" or "Can you say more about that?" to help continue a discussion and give it greater depth.

- Affirm others' responses with comments such as "Great" or "Thanks" or "Good insight"—especially if it's the first time someone has spoken during the group session.

- Monitor your own contributions. If you are doing most of the talking, back off so that you do not train the group to listen rather than speak up.

- Remember that you do not have all the answers. Your job is to keep the discussion going and encourage participation.

Managing the Session

- Honor the time schedule. If a session is running longer than expected, get consensus from the group before continuing beyond the agreed-upon ending time.

- Involve group members in various aspects of the group session, such as saying prayers or reading the Scripture.
- Note that the session guides sometimes call for breaking into smaller groups or pairs. This gives everyone a chance to speak and participate fully. Mix up the groups; don't let the same people pair up for every activity.
- As always in discussions that may involve personal sharing, confidentiality is essential. Group members should never pass along stories that have been shared in the group. Remind the group members at each session: confidentiality is crucial to the success of this study.

The Oldest Question in the Universe

Planning the Session

Session Goals

Through this session's discussion and activities, participants will be encouraged to:

- reflect on their identities and the identities they convey to others;
- explore Jesus' identity and what it means for him to be fully human and fully divine;
- examine how they have grown through their various personas or "reincarnations" during their lives;
- consider how memory shapes identity, and how we remember our identities as God's children and followers of Christ.

Preparation

- Familiarize yourself with the premise of *Doctor Who* and some of the key characters and themes.
- Read and reflect on the first chapter of Matt Rawle's *The Salvation of Doctor Who*.
- Read through this Leader Guide session in its entirety to familiarize yourself with the material being covered.
- Read and reflect on the following Scriptures:
  - ❏ Mark 8:27–38
  - ❏ Matthew 4:1–11
  - ❏ Mark 14:32–42
  - ❏ Philippians 2:5–11
  - ❏ Ezekiel 36:24–32
  - ❏ Romans 6:1–11
  - ❏ Galatians 2:16–21
  - ❏ Genesis 32:22–32
  - ❏ Matthew 16:13–20
- Make sure that you have a markerboard or large sheet of paper on which you can record group members' ideas.
- Have a Bible for every participant, along with paper and pens for taking notes.

OPENING ACTIVITY AND PRAYER
(10 MINUTES)

As participants arrive, welcome them to this study. When most are present, consider this question that Matt Rawle asks: "If I asked you to write a three-sentence bio about yourself, what would you say? How do you describe your identity?" Have each participant answer this question on a note card. Give everyone a few minutes to write their bios, then collect and shuffle the cards. Read aloud each short bio and have the group guess to whom each belongs. Discuss:

- What did you learn about the members of this group that you didn't know before?
- What surprised you about these bios? Might you have described anyone differently?
- Think about the bio you wrote. Is this the identity that you convey to others? Why, or why not?

Then have participants discuss their familiarity with *Doctor Who*. It is OK if some have never seen a single episode and have no idea what a Dalek looks like. But if some participants are fans of the show, have them give their fellow participants a better understanding of the show by discussing some of the following:

- who the Doctor is;
- what a companion is and what the Doctor's traveling companions do;
- why they think *Doctor Who* has endured for so long and is beloved on both sides of the Atlantic;
- why a show such as *Doctor Who* would inspire a Bible study.

OPENING PRAYER

Lord, as we begin this study, give us wisdom, patience, and humility. Thank you for this group and for the opportunity for us to come together and reflect on what we, as Christians, can learn from popular culture and science fiction. Bless our time together that we may learn from Scripture, from story, and from one another. Amen.

WATCH DVD SEGMENT
(10 MINUTES)

STUDY AND DISCUSSION
(30–35 MINUTES)

<u>Note:</u> Discussion helps and questions that correspond to Chapter One: "The Oldest Question in the Universe" are provided below. If you have more time in your session, or want to include additional discussion and activities to your time, see "Additional Options for Bible Study and Discussion" at the end of this section, listed after the Closing Activity and Prayer.

Who Is the Doctor?

(See *The Salvation of Doctor Who,* pages 22–25.)

Read aloud or summarize for the group:

Rawle writes, "Identity can be a tricky thing to explain." He notes that, in the eyes of his enemies the Daleks, the Doctor is a predator, or a terrorist. But to those who fear and have been hurt by the Daleks—who are cruel and known for feeling no compassion or remorse—the Doctor is a freedom fighter.

For discussion:

- Read Mark 8:27–38, where Jesus asks his disciples, "Who do you say that I am?"
- What identities for Jesus had people proposed?
- Why, do you think, did they associate these identities with Jesus?
- Peter identifies Jesus as "the Christ." What does this identity mean for Jesus and his followers?

- If Jesus were to ask you, "Who do you say that I am?" how would you answer?

Having Two Hearts

(See The Salvation of Doctor Who, pages 25–30.)

Read aloud or summarize for the group:

Rawle relates a *Doctor Who* episode in which the Doctor, who is a Time Lord, alters his DNA to become human. In becoming human, the Doctor took on human "biases and missteps, losing his ability to rise above bigotry and fear."

Our Christian faith affirms that, in the person of Jesus, God became human. The difference between Jesus and the Doctor (among other things) is that while Jesus was fully human, he also was fully divine. Though he was saddled with certain human limitations and vulnerabilities, he retained his divine knowledge and power.

For discussion:

- What does it mean that, in Jesus, God was fully human?
- In what ways did Jesus experience the limitations and vulnerabilities that we experience as human beings?
- What risks did God take by becoming human, and particularly by beginning life as an infant?
- How, do you think, did the fact that Jesus also was fully divine affect his life as a human being?
- What does the fact that God became fully human say about God's relationship with us and about how we relate to God?

(Refer to the following Scriptures as a part of your discussion: Matthew 4:1–11; Mark 14:32–42; Philippians 2:5–11.)

Read aloud or summarize for the group:

One of the Doctor's most extraordinary characteristics is that he has two hearts. Rawle suggests that, as Christians, we also have a second heart, in a manner of speaking: "Being in Christ means that our heart works together with Christ's and with each other."

For discussion:

- How does your heart work "together with Christ's"?
- How are our hearts, through Christ, joined to those of other Christians?

I Never Forget a Face

(See *The Salvation of Doctor Who*, pages 30–33.)

Read aloud or summarize for the group:

One of the Doctor's most remarkable characteristics is his ability to regenerate. When he is on the verge of death, his cells rearrange to create a new body. His new body is different not only in appearance but also in taste and attitude. The Doctor's companions sometimes struggle with the question of whether the regenerated Doctor is the same person they'd known before.

For discussion:

- Like the Doctor, we are always growing and changing. When you look back at early pictures of yourself, do you see the same person you are today, or do you see another person entirely?

- Compare yourself now to yourself from another period in your life. Do you see yourself as the same person now as then or as someone entirely different?
- If you from ten or twenty years ago were to see you today, what would surprise your past self most about you today?

Run, You Clever Boy, and Remember

(See *The Salvation of Doctor Who,* pages 33–37.)

Read aloud or summarize for the group:

Over the course of our lives our appearances change, our personalities and perspectives change, and our cells die off and are replaced. For the Doctor, these changes are more extreme. He periodically regenerates, taking on an entirely new body.

Galatians 2:20, which says, "I have been crucified with Christ and I no longer live, but Christ lives in me. And the life that I now live in my body, I live by faith, indeed, by the faithfulness of God's Son, who loved me and gave himself for me."

Rawle writes, "Whatever it is you consider 'I' to be, whatever you see in your mind's eye when you say your name, whatever that image is, the point is for 'I' to be crucified so that Christ may live within us. In other words, my prayer is that 'I' reflects Jesus Christ. The 'I' has been redeemed."

For discussion:

- What is it that makes you, you? What remains constant through all the changes?
- Would you agree with Rawle that identity is rooted in memory? Why, or why not?

- What does it mean for us to be "crucified with Christ," for some part of us to die and be replaced by Christ living within us?
- What died or changed within you when you became a Christian or matured in your faith?

Then read (or re-read) Romans 6:1–11. Ask:

- What do you think the Apostle Paul (the author of these verses) means when he says that we were "buried together" with Christ or that we are "united together in a death like his"? How have you "died" with Christ?
- How are we "united together" in Christ's resurrection? What must happen before we can experience resurrection?

CLOSING ACTIVITY
(5 MINUTES)

Ask the group:

- What is one thing you learned from this session that you didn't know before? (Participants could name something they learned about Scripture; something they learned about one another; or even something interesting they learned about *Doctor Who*.)
- What is one important truth about God's identity that you will take away from this session?
- What is one important truth about your identity as a follower of Christ that you will take away from this session?

If time permits:

Invite participants to imagine they can hop into the TARDIS and travel one week into the future. What would they like to have learned or accomplished during this coming week? Encourage participants to make a personal goal for themselves this week.

For example, one possible goal could be making a commitment to join one's heart to Christ (see "Having Two Hearts") in a particular way, such as by spending time each morning reading and reflecting on Scripture. Another could be to allow part of oneself—such as a grudge or an obsession—to die so that he or she could be made new ("I Remember, Therefore I Am").

Provide paper and pen for each person so participants can write down these goals as a reminder for the week. Some may want to share their goals with the group.

Note: when it comes to goal setting, some people find it helpful to use the SMART acronym as a guideline, which states that goals should be:

- *S*pecific: Goals should not be vague or abstract.
- *M*easurable: There should be some objective way to say, "Yes, I accomplished this goal" or "No, I did not."
- *A*chievable: They should be able to complete their goals in a week's time.
- *R*elevant: Their goals should relate to the content of this session.
- *T*ime limited: Goals should not require more than a week's time.

CLOSING PRAYER

Lord, thank you for this time we've had together. We are grateful that we see glimpses of you in popular culture and that we are able to use the story of the Doctor as a tool with

*which we can explore your eternal truths. Bless us as we go
from here. Remind us of the identities we have in you and
give us the strength and wisdom to be faithful to them. In
Jesus' name we pray. Amen.*

ADDITIONAL OPTIONS FOR BIBLE STUDY AND DISCUSSION

The Oldest Question (15 minutes)
(See *The Salvation of Doctor Who,* pages 38–41.)

Activity:

Below is a list of names of people whose birth names are
different from their given, or chosen, names. Write the pairs of
names below on a markerboard, but scramble them so that it
isn't obvious which name goes with which. Challenge participants to match the person's original name on the left with the
appropriate new name on the right.

• Sarai	Sarah
• Jacob	Israel
• Daniel	Belteshazzar
• Simon	Peter
• Cassius Clay	Muhammad Ali
• Stefani Germonotta	Lady Gaga
• Reginald Dwight	Elton John
• Caryn Johnson	Whoopi Goldberg
• Peter Gene Hernandez	Bruno Mars

<u>Optional:</u> If time permits, and if members of your group have
children, invite them to tell the stories behind their children's

names, talking about anything that is special or significant about these names. How much thought did they put into naming the children? Did it cause them any stress or tension?

Read aloud or summarize for the group:

Most names have some sort of a story behind them. For the Doctor, the story is that his name is unknown to all but himself and River Song, his wife. In Scripture, we encounter many names of great significance. Let's look at these examples:

- Genesis 32:22–32
- Matthew 16:13–20 (You might also want to look at any footnotes.)

For discussion:

- What is the story behind the name of the people of Israel? What does this name say about the people's relationship with God?
- What is the story behind Peter's name? What does this name say about Peter and his later role as a leader of the church?
- If God were to give you a new name to reflect your relationship with God, your gifts, or your calling, what might it be and why?

Activity (15 minutes)

Twelve actors have portrayed the Doctor since the show's debut in 1963. And each of the Doctor's twelve regenerations has his own strengths and idiosyncrasies. Rawle gives a summary of each of the Doctors on pages 31–32.

Many of us experience regenerations, even if they aren't as substantial as the Doctor's. Give the members of your group about five minutes to make a list of a few of their different "selfs" or "incarnations" with dates and a list of attributes. (For example: "The First Phil, 1976–1979: limited ability to communicate, heavily dependent on parents" or "The Fourth Jennifer, 1988–1991: a beast on the softball diamond but hampered by an unhealthy obsession with the New Kids on the Block.") Allow everyone to present one or two of their regenerations, then ask:

- What role did your faith play in these regenerations?

Divide participants into three teams. Have each team read one of the following Scriptures and discuss what their Scriptures have to say about regeneration:

- Ezekiel 36:24–32
- Romans 6:1–11
- Galatians 2:16–21

After the teams have had time to read and discuss their Scriptures, have each team summarize its verses for the others, explaining how the Scriptures relate to regeneration. Following these summaries, discuss:

- How is regeneration a part of who we are as children of God and followers of Christ?

Nicknames (10 minutes)

Activity:

Chances are, some members of your group have picked up nicknames at some point in their lives. Invite participants to name these nicknames. Ask volunteers to tell the stories behind their nicknames. Did they, like Peter, get a nickname from someone who saw a particular quality in them? Or, like the Doctor, did they choose a name for themselves that happened to catch on?

About each nickname, ask:

- How or why did this name catch on?
- How long did the name persist? Do people still refer to you by this name?
- What, in your opinion, makes for a good nickname?

Have everyone write his or her name on a slip of paper. Collect the slips and put them into a container. Ask each participant to draw a slip from the container. Every person should come up with a nickname for the person whose name he or she drew from the container. This nickname should be based on some way in which God has gifted the person or some way in which he or she has served or contributed to God's people.

Session 2

GOD AND TIME AND GOD'S TIME

PLANNING THE SESSION

Session Goals

Through this session's discussion and activities, participants will be encouraged to:

- reflect on the role that time and time-keeping play in our lives;
- consider the difference between God's understanding of time and human understandings of time;
- examine the ways in which God enters our time line;
- question our assumptions about how God is at work in our world;
- consider how God's kingdom is already among us.

Preparation

- Familiarize yourself with the premise of *Doctor Who* and some of the key characters and themes.

- Read and reflect on the second chapter of Matt Rawle's *The Salvation of Doctor Who*.
- Read through this Leader Guide session in its entirety to familiarize yourself with the material being covered.
- Read and reflect on the following Scriptures:
  - ❏ Matthew 17:1–13
  - ❏ Luke 17:20–21
  - ❏ John 1:43–51
- Make sure that you have a markerboard or large sheet of paper on which you can record group members' ideas.
- Have a Bible available for each participant, along with paper and pens for taking notes.

OPENING ACTIVITY AND PRAYER (10 MINUTES)

Ask participants to close their eyes and to imagine going through their day without having anything to keep time—no clocks, no watches, no cell phones, and so forth. Have them start imagining at the beginning of the day then go through each part of their daily routine.

After a few minutes of imagining, ask:

- What is the first challenge you would likely encounter while going through the day without a clock or watch? What do you think would be most difficult about not knowing what time it was?
- Do you think that you would be able to make it through the average day without some sort of watch or clock? Why, or why not?

- What are the benefits of time-keeping devices? In what ways might they be detrimental? Are there any drawbacks to putting so much of our lives on a schedule?
- Rawle says, "Time is a great example of God's grace." He describes it as a gift. Does time feel like a blessing or gift to you, or does it feel like more of a burden?
- How would thinking of time as a gift of God's grace affect how you manage your time?

OPENING PRAYER

Lord, as we continue this study, give us wisdom, patience, and humility. Thank you for this group and for the opportunity for us to come together and reflect on what we, as Christians, can learn from popular culture and science fiction. Bless our time together that we may learn from Scripture, from story, and from one another. Amen.

WATCH DVD SEGMENT
(10 MINUTES)

STUDY AND DISCUSSION
(30–35 MINUTES)

Note: Discussion helps and questions that correspond to Chapter Two: "God and Time and God's Time" are provided below. If you have more time in your session, or want to include additional discussion and activities to your time, see "Additional Options for Bible Study and Discussion" at the end of this section, listed after the Closing Activity and Prayer.

An Uncaused Effect

(See *The Salvation of Doctor Who,* pages 50–54.)

Read aloud or summarize for the group:

Because of the wibbly-wobbliness of the time line, typical understandings of cause and effect don't exactly fit with many of the story arcs in *Doctor Who.* In the episode "Blink," the Doctor and his companion are stuck in 1969 without the TARDIS (the vehicle they would normally use to travel through space and time) and must communicate with characters living in what had been the present but is now more than forty years into the future. The Doctor explains in this episode that time is not linear and cannot be reduced to a series of causes and effects.

Rawle writes,

We often assume that time flows in one direction from cause to effect, but this cannot be the case. Let's assume that every effect has a cause, or "A" causes "B," which causes "C," and so on. For example, imagine you are at a dinner party. Someone tells a really great joke about a pickle, a Dalmatian, and a funny-smelling shoe. You laugh so hard you knock your water glass off the table with your elbow, and it shatters into pieces. Cause and effect would look like this: You laugh at the joke (A), you knock the glass with your elbow (B), and then the glass shatters when it hits the floor (C). The problem is, if you rewind the clock you discover that, at some point, you run across an uncaused effect. The joke made you laugh, but who told the joke? Who told the joke to them? So on and so forth. If you look closely, you'll eventually discover the moment in which something happened from nothing. It is specifically *not* the case that our world moves *only* from cause to effect.

So, what does an uncaused effect look like? The church sometimes calls them miracles. It looks like water being turned into wine. It looks like feeding five thousand people from a young boy's lunch of fish and loaves. It looks like Jesus being transfigured on the mountain talking with Moses and Elijah in defiance of our simple cause-to-effect world. God is the uncaused effect—action with no beginning and no end; and when God enters into our world, we are reminded of how marvelously and strangely beautiful God's world is. When we worship a risen Lord, when we live as if our story ends with everlasting life, the rules of the world do not apply.

For discussion:

- Why does Rawle compare biblical miracles to the "uncaused" effects that he describes in *Doctor Who*?
- What is your experience with "uncaused effects" or miracles? Have you witnessed or experienced an event that you would describe as miraculous?
  - ❑ What do these miracles tell us about what is possible through God?
  - ❑ What do these miracles tell us about God's priorities?

Moving at the Speed of Salvation

(See *The Salvation of Doctor Who*, pages 54–58.)

Read aloud or summarize for the group:

In *The Salvation of Doctor Who*, Rawle mentions a two-part *Doctor Who* episode in which the Doctor encounters a creature that doesn't fit his understanding of how the universe works. This being has existed since before the beginning of the universe. In the Doctor's mind, this is an impossibility. He says:

I believe I haven't seen everything, I don't know. It's funny, isn't it? The things you make up. The rules. If that thing had said it came from beyond the universe, I'd believe it, but before the universe? Impossible. Doesn't fit my rule. Still, that's why I keep traveling. To be proved wrong.[1]

Activity:

Divide participants into teams of three or four. Challenge participants to think of and discuss a time when they witnessed or experienced something that broke a rule or assumption they had about how the world works. For example, maybe someone had rules in his or her mind for how people from a certain part of town or part of the country think and act until he or she met someone who broke those rules.

Have them discuss:

- How did these experiences affect your faith and your understanding of how God works?
- How did these experiences affect how you see and understand other people?
- Read John 1:43–51. Discuss (either in teams or as a whole group): What rule did Nathaniel have? How did Jesus force Nathaniel to reconsider this rule?

The Cross and Relativity
(See *The Salvation of Doctor Who,* pages 58–62.)

For discussion:

- Think about your relationship with Christ. Can you identify one moment when you accepted God's grace through Christ, or do you think your relationship with him grew and developed over time?

Read aloud or summarize for the group:

Rawle proposes the idea that—through Christ's life, death, and resurrection—God reconciled all things, including time, "so that time itself is simply an agent of the gospel." In other words, Christ meant salvation not only for his contemporaries but also for those who had come before and those who came along later, including us. So salvation, to borrow the Doctor's term, is "time-y wimey."

Activity:

With this in mind, give each participant a sheet of paper and have him or her create a time line. This time line should include events—past and present (and possibly future)—that were integral to their story of salvation. Participants could follow their time lines back to the time of Jesus or even back to the days of the ancient Israelites. They could include events from their families' pasts or events from their personal lives.

Give everyone a few minutes to work, then ask participants to present their time lines and to talk about the events they included. Encourage them to discuss what role each event played in the story of their faith.

The Eternal Now
(See *The Salvation of Doctor Who*, pages 62–65.)

For discussion:

- Imagine that you, like the Doctor, had a vehicle that could travel through time and space, covering light years and centuries in a matter of moments. How would your perspective on life and time change? How would your priorities change?

- Rawle says that, for the Doctor, the time is always now. The same is true for God. Rawle says that God lives in the present. Read Luke 17:20–21. Discuss:
  - ❏ What do you think Jesus means when he says that the kingdom of God is among us already?
  - ❏ How do you see signs of God's kingdom in your world today?
  - ❏ What are you doing now to show God's love and do the work of God's kingdom?

CLOSING ACTIVITY
(5 MINUTES)

Ask the group:

- What is one thing you learned from this session that you didn't know before? (Participants could name something they learned about Scripture; something they learned about one another; or even something interesting they learned about *Doctor Who*.)
- What is one important truth about how God intervenes in our world that you will take away from this session?

If time permits:

Invite participants to imagine they can hop into the TARDIS and travel one week into the future. What would they like to have learned or accomplished during this coming week? Encourage participants to make a personal goal for themselves this week, perhaps using the SMART acronym as a guideline. (See page 19 in Session 1.)

For instance, a participant might decide to keep a journal of all the ways he or she notices God entering his or her time line in the coming week. Or, one might make a goal of doing the work of God's kingdom in a particular way, such as by volunteering with a ministry or organization that needs help.

Provide paper and pen for each person so participants can write down these goals as a reminder for the week. Some may want to share their goals with the group.

CLOSING PRAYER

Lord, thank you for this time we've had together and for all that you have taught us through discussion and through our exploration of Scripture, science fiction, and pop culture. Bless us as we go from here. Remind us of the identities we have in you and give us the strength and wisdom to be faithful to them. In Jesus' name we pray. Amen.

ADDITIONAL OPTIONS FOR BIBLE STUDY AND DISCUSSION

When Time Began (15–20 minutes)
(See *The Salvation of Doctor Who,* page 45.)

Read the text box "When Time Began," which appears on page 45 in *The Salvation of Doctor Who*. Rawle looks at the tension that sometimes arises between religious beliefs and scientific findings. Ask:

- Do you feel that your Christian faith is at odds with scientific understandings of biology or cosmology? Why, or why not?

- Rawle reconciles the scientific understanding of life on earth with Scripture. What common ground exists between science and Scripture? How might science and Scripture be at odds?
- What can science teach us about God and how God is at work in the universe?
- How might Scripture and our faith inform our understanding of science?

Invite participants to name questions they have about the origin of the cosmos or the origin and development of life on earth. List these on a markerboard or large sheet of paper. For each question on your list, ask:

- How important is it to our faith that we answer this question?
- Where might you look for answers to this question?
- What can this question teach us about God and the universe God created?

The Big Bang (15 minutes)
(See *The Salvation of Doctor Who,* pages 46–50.)

Activity:

Go around the room and ask each person to make a future prediction about the person sitting to his or her right. This prediction could be for one year into the future or decades into the future and could be something personal or something more general, depending on how well the members know one another. Participants should stick to making positive prognostications.

After everyone has had a chance to make predictions, ask:

- On what basis did you make your predictions?
- How did your knowledge of your partner influence your predictions?

Read aloud or summarize for the group:

In this chapter Rawle asks, "Does God know the future?" (page 48 in *The Salvation of Doctor Who*). He concludes that, while God doesn't necessarily see into the future, God knows what we will do in the future because God knows us so well—better than we know ourselves.

Rawle writes,

> If God knows us better than we know ourselves, can we ever surprise God? I think so. God knows the future in the sense that God knows all that is possible, but there is room for surprise. Think of it this way. God knows every possible way to get from Los Angeles to New York, but whether I take a right or a left out of my driveway at the beginning of my road trip is undetermined. Have you ever tried to surprise God for the good? Maybe you always worry about money. Try surprising God by putting your worry away (see Matthew 6:25). Maybe you never begin your mornings with prayer. What a pleasant surprise to talk to God first thing before the sun rises! God knows us better than we know ourselves.

For discussion:

- God knows where the story is headed, and yet God graciously invites us into the story as active participants. What is one way you can surprise God in the coming week?

THE SONIC SCREWDRIVER IS MIGHTIER THAN THE SWORD

PLANNING THE SESSION

Session Goals

Through this session's discussion and activities, participants will be encouraged to:

- consider their own definitions of *good* and consider ways in which those perspectives might miss the mark;
- examine where God draws the line between good and bad;
- wrestle with the topic of forgiveness and reflect on whom they need to forgive;
- consider how remembering is central to who we are as followers of Christ;

- explore Jesus' identity and what it means for him to be fully human and fully divine;
- identify ways they can respond to the evil they encounter.

Preparation

- Familiarize yourself with the premise of *Doctor Who* and some of the key characters and themes.
- Read and reflect on the third chapter of Matt Rawle's *The Salvation of Doctor Who*.
- Read through this Leader Guide session in its entirety to familiarize yourself with the material being covered.
- Read and reflect on the following Scriptures:
  - ❏ Genesis 3:1–24
  - ❏ Ezekiel 36:24–32
  - ❏ Matthew 18:21–35
  - ❏ Matthew 25:31–46
  - ❏ Luke 15:11–32
  - ❏ Luke 24:13–35
  - ❏ John 20:11–18
  - ❏ John 21:1–14
  - ❏ Romans 7:13–20
- Make sure that you have a markerboard or large sheet of paper on which you can record group members' ideas.
- Have a Bible for every participant, along with paper and pens for taking notes.

OPENING ACTIVITY AND PRAYER (10 MINUTES)

Open by asking participants to name some of the great villains from fiction and literature. List their ideas on a markerboard or sheet of paper. Once you have a pretty good list, ask the group:

- What makes them villains? What makes these villains great villains?
- Why are villains important to fictional narratives? What would stories lose if there were no villains?
- Do you sympathize with any of the villains on this list? How might some of the stories we referenced change if we looked at them from the villains' perspective?
- What can we learn from villains about the world? About ourselves? About God?

Opening Prayer

Lord, thank you for what we've learned so far in this study and give us wisdom and humility as we examine the topics of evil, conflict, and forgiveness. Bless this time we have together so that we can learn from one another, from Scripture, and from your Holy Spirit. Work within us that we might grow in spirit through our discussions and reflections. In Jesus' name, amen.

WATCH DVD SEGMENT
(10 MINUTES)

Study and Discussion
(30–35 MINUTES)

<u>Note:</u> Discussion helps and questions that correspond to Chapter Three: "The Sonic Screwdriver Is Mightier than the Sword" are provided below. If you have more time in your session, or want to include additional discussion and activities to your time, see

"Additional Options for Bible Study and Discussion" at the end of this section, listed after the Closing Activity and Prayer.

Good Guys and Bad Guys

Activity:

As a group, brainstorm a list of famous rivalries. These could be sports rivals (Barcelona and Real Madrid, Bears and Packers); they could be corporate rivals (Coke and Pepsi, Apple and Amazon); they could be musicians and entertainers that are in the same genre and often are compared to one another.

Once you have four or so pairs listed, divide participants into teams of three or four. Have each team select one pair of rivals. Teams should designate one rival as the good guy(s) and another as the bad guy(s). They should come up with a reason why one rival is good and the other bad, even if this reason isn't completely fair or rational. After a few minutes, invite teams to explain their reasoning. Then discuss:

- What are some situations where it's clear who is in the wrong and who is in the right?
- What are some situations where it isn't so clear?
- Read Matthew 25:31–46. In this Scripture, the "Human One" (CEB) or "Son of Man" (NRSV) separates the nations as a shepherd would separate sheep and goats. By what criteria does the Human One or Son of Man separate the righteous from the wicked?
- Rawle writes that, while it is tempting to think of some people as sheep and others as goats (usually thinking of ourselves as the sheep and those with whom we disagree as goats), in actuality "the dividing line runs right through

our own soul." How do you feel the tension between good and evil at play in your soul?

Good versus Evil
(See *The Salvation of Doctor Who*, page 70.)

Activity:

Divide participants into teams of three or four. Have each team pick one of the villains from the list you made as a part of the opening activity.

While some villains are truly evil and devoid of any rationality or remorse, most villains can justify their actions, and many are convinced that they are in the right. Challenge each group to look at things from the villains' point of view, considering the following:

- How might the villains' view of the world and understanding of what is right differ from that of the hero (or the author, reader, or viewer)?
- How might the villain justify his or her actions and beliefs? Are any of these justifications legitimate?
- What makes your villain a villain? Why does the author, reader, or viewer side with the protagonist and against the villain?

After a few minutes, ask each team to name the villain it chose and to summarize what they discussed.

For discussion:

Rawle writes,

"Sometimes our definition of *good* really misses the mark. That's the problem with sin." For what reasons might different people end up with different definitions of *good*? What influences our understandings of *good* and *bad*?

- How do you determine what is good?
- When have you had to change your understanding of what is good? What caused this change?
- Read Romans 7:13–20. Paul writes in verse 15, "I don't know what I'm doing, because I don't do what I want to do. Instead, I do the thing that I hate." When have you acted in ways that you knew to be wrong?
- For what reasons do we act in ways that are contrary to what we know to be good and right?

Exterminate! and Delete!
(See *The Salvation of Doctor Who,* pages 71–75.)

Read aloud or summarize for the group:

The Daleks are possibly the Doctor's best known, most dangerous, and most important adversaries. Daleks were the product of an evil genius named Davros who created the creatures in an effort to bring an end to a thousand-year war. Davros's creations ended up being nearly indestructible and bent on destroying anything or anyone who was not one of their kind.

Daleks are ruthless, and they aren't the sort of villains that viewers can sympathize with. Nonetheless they are motivated by what they consider to be good. In the case of the Daleks, they sincerely believe that the universe would be better off under their complete control.

For discussion:

- Read Genesis 3:1–24. How do the first humans in this Scripture try to take control? What are the effects?

- Rawle describes this sin as an "act of idolatry"? Why were Adam and Eve's actions idolatrous?
- How have you, like Adam and Eve, tried to take control of a situation even though it meant disobeying God or rejecting instructions from someone wiser than you?

The Silence of a Weeping Angel
(See *The Salvation of Doctor Who,* pages 83–87.)

Read aloud or summarize for the group:

The Silence, one of the Doctor's most frightening adversaries, steal their victims' identities by destroying their memories. As Christians, remembering our story is essential to who we are and what we do.

Rawle relates the story of Jesus appearing on the shore to his disciples following his resurrection, at a time when Simon Peter is acting as though he'd forgotten that Jesus lived. Peter was not the only one who struggled to recognize Jesus following the Resurrection.

Activity:

- Divide participants into three teams, and have each team look at one of the following Resurrection Scriptures:
  - ❏ Luke 24:13–35
  - ❏ John 20:11–18
  - ❏ John 21:1–14

Each team should identify what Jesus does in its Scripture that causes his followers to recognize him as the risen Christ. What is significant about this act that triggers their memories? Ask each team to summarize its Scripture, to explain what Jesus does to stimulate his followers' memories, and to talk about the significance of this act.

Compare what Jesus does and says in these Scriptures to the rituals and practices you listed earlier. Then ask:

- What are some other examples of events or actions that help you remember your identity as a child of God and a follower of Christ? What are some rituals and practices that help us do this? (Examples include Holy Communion, Advent candles, remembrance of baptism rituals, and so forth.)
- Why is it important to daily remember and revisit our identity in Christ?

CLOSING ACTIVITY
(5 MINUTES)

Ask the group:

- What is one thing you learned from this session that you didn't know before? (Participants could name something they learned about Scripture; something they learned about one another; or even something interesting they learned about *Doctor Who*.)
- What is one important truth about how we understand "good" and "bad" that you will take away from this session?
- What is one important truth about grace and forgiveness that you will take away from this session?

If time permits:

Invite participants to imagine they can hop into the TARDIS and travel one week into the future. What would they like to have learned or accomplished during this coming week? Encourage participants to make a personal goal for themselves this week, perhaps using the SMART acronym as a guideline. (See page 19 in Session 1.)

Possible goals this week might include making an effort to get to know better someone they normally don't get along with or forgiving someone whom they have not yet had the courage to forgive (see "The Tough Pill of Grace" and "The Master of Rejection").

- Provide paper and pen for each person so participants can write down these goals as a reminder for the week. Some may want to share their goals with the group.

CLOSING PRAYER

Lord, thank you for this time we've had together to reflect on the presence of evil and the villains we encounter in our world. Bless us as we go from here. Give us the strength to respond to evil in our midst and, by the power of your Holy Spirit, to redeem and transform it. Give us the wisdom to see things from the perspectives of our enemies and adversaries and to recognize situations where we might be the villains. We pray all these things in Jesus' name. Amen.

ADDITIONAL OPTIONS FOR BIBLE STUDY AND DISCUSSION

The Master of Rejection (15 minutes)
(See *The Salvation of Doctor Who*, pages 75–79.)

Read aloud or summarize for the group:

This chapter is all about the Doctor's enemies. Perhaps one of Jesus' most difficult teachings comes from his Sermon on the Mount, where he says, "Love your enemies and pray for those who harass you" (Matthew 5:44).

The Master, a childhood friend of the Doctor's who was driven to madness, may be the most sympathetic of *Doctor Who* adversaries. Rawle relates an episode in which the master comes close to reaching his goal of taking over the earth and enslaving humanity. After foiling the Master's plot, the Doctor offers his old friend forgiveness—an act we don't always expect from our heroes.

For discussion:

- Who are some other fictional heroes who are notable for responding to their enemies with grace? Who are some heroes who might look upon grace and forgiveness as weakness?
- Read Peter's question about forgiveness and Jesus' response from Matthew 18:21–35. Jesus instructs his followers to forgive those who have wronged them many times. What does it look like to forgive someone over and over?
- In the parable of the unforgiving servant, it is very obvious that the servant is in the wrong. What might be a more subtle example of how we neglect to show others the grace that has been shown to us?
- What is most difficult about Jesus' teachings on for-giveness?
- Is there a difference between forgiving someone and forgetting or excusing what that person has done? If so, what?

Activity:

Hand out slips of paper or index cards. Ask participants to spend a few minutes reflecting on barriers that keep them from forgiving those who have hurt them. Have everyone write one of these barriers on their card or slip of paper—or, alternatively, to jot it down on a notes or reminders app on his or her phone— and keep it with them in their wallet, purse, Bible, or other place where they will see it often. This should serve as a reminder of the barrier that often stands in the way of their forgiving someone and present itself as an opportunity to pray and ask God to help them move toward forgiveness.

Choose Your Villain (10 minutes)

Activity:

Ask participants to think about the various *Doctor Who* villains that Rawle discusses in this chapter and to select the villain with whom they identify the most. (Fans of the show might also consider other adversaries that Rawle doesn't mention.) For instance, someone might relate most to the Daleks because he or she has a need to always be in control. Someone might feel a connection to the Cybermen, whose obsession with perfection has left her or him callous. Someone else might compare him- or herself to the Master, driven by jealousy and arrogance.

Have participants pair off and talk about which villains they relate to and why. Then invite volunteers to explain the reasoning behind their choosing a particular villain.

Ask:

- Think about the traits you share with the villains you named. Are these characteristics ones that you would like to eliminate (such as arrogance), or are they neutral characteristics that can be good or bad depending on context (such as ambition)?

- In much of popular culture, the line separating heroes from villains is clear. In real life the boundary between the two tends to be blurred. Are there situations in which you might be considered a villain?

- Why is it important to look at the world from others' perspectives, and particularly from the perspectives of those you might consider enemies?

The Tough Pill of Grace (15 minutes)
(See *The Salvation of Doctor Who,* pages 79–83.)

Rawle mentions that the Master—himself one of the Doctor's greatest adversaries—"is disgusted by the Doctor's grace toward his enemies." Ask:

- Can you think of a time when you were disgusted by grace, when you felt that someone deserved a greater punishment or was not worthy of the forgiveness they received? (This may include being upset by someone getting off too easy or by a friend letting something go that you felt they should not have.)

The biblical story most associated with this attitude of being disgusted by grace is Jesus' parable about a father and two sons. Read this parable in Luke 15:11–32. Discuss:

- To whom do you relate most in this story? Why?
- Was the father in this story right to forgive his youngest son so readily? Why, or why not?

- Was the oldest son right to be upset by his father's grace? Why, or why not?
- Traditionally this parable is called the parable of the prodigal son. If you had no prior knowledge of that name and were to give this parable a name based on what it teaches about grace and forgiveness, what name would you choose?
- While Jesus' teachings on forgiveness are clear, we should not expect it to be easy to follow the example of the father in this parable. There are many situations in which forgiveness is—and probably should be—a struggle. Moreover, forgiving someone is not the same as excusing what that person has done. How do you know when you've truly forgiven someone? (Possible answers include: You don't allow what happened to control you; you no longer hold a grudge.)

The Redemption of Evil (15 minutes)
(See *The Salvation of Doctor Who,* pages 88–91.)

Divide participants into three teams. Rawle mentions three ways that we might understand the existence of evil. Assign one of these ways to each team:

- Evil is the result of sin, a separation of God and humanity.
- Evil is a spiritual force that stands opposed to God.
- Evil is nothing but the negation of good.

Rawle elaborates on each of these in "The Redemption of section. Teams should read through what Rawle has to say about their way of understanding evil. Then, based on this understanding, they should come up with three or more ways that we can respond to evil. For example, the team considering evil as a separation of God and humanity could think of ways to bring humanity closer to God. The team considering evil as a spiritual force could identify ways to strengthen ourselves spiritually. The team considering evil as the negation of good could look at how we could transform or redeem that which is evil. It is important that each team keep in mind that God empowers us to respond to evil. It is not something we can do on our own.

Give the teams about five minutes to read and discuss, then invite each to name its ways to respond to evil. Record all three teams' ideas on a markerboard or large sheet of paper and discuss how members can utilize these responses in their own lives.

Session 4

Bigger on the Inside

Planning the Session

Session Goals

Through this session's discussion and activities, participants will be encouraged to:

- reflect on God as the Trinity, what it means for God to be three and one at the same time, and how relationship is essential to God's being;
- consider how their understanding of who God is and what God does has grown;
- examine the topic of evangelism and how God calls us to be evangelists;
- identify ways that they, individually and as a congregation, have been successful as evangelists and ways in which they could improve;

- affirm the importance of hope and look for ways to surround people with beauty as they travel the difficult path from suffering to hope;
- consider Holy Communion as their "own little time machine."

Preparation

- Read and reflect on the fourth chapter of Matt Rawle's *The Salvation of Doctor Who*.
- Read through this Leader Guide session in its entirety to familiarize yourself with the material being covered.
- Read and reflect on the following Scriptures:
  - ❏ Genesis 18:1–15
  - ❏ Job 38–42
  - ❏ Matthew 3:13–17
  - ❏ Matthew 28:18–20
  - ❏ Mark 1:16–20
  - ❏ Luke 22:14–20
  - ❏ John 14:15–17
  - ❏ 2 Corinthians 13:13
  - ❏ Philippians 2:5–8
- Make sure that you have a markerboard or large sheet of paper on which you can record group members' ideas.
- Have a Bible for every participant, along with paper and pens for taking notes.
- Provide, or have participants provide, refreshments for "Our Own Little Time Machine."

Opening Activity and Prayer
(10 minutes)

To open your time together, ask participants to think about—but not talk about—objects or buildings or vehicles that are so amazing that they almost defy explanation. This might include something that is extravagant or that uses cutting-edge technology; it could also include something common that we often take for granted. (For example, someone may be amazed by the fact that keys and locks work as well as they do.)

After everyone has had time to think of something, invite one person to name something he or she thought of. Another person should then try to one-up the first person's example by naming something that he or she considers even more amazing. Each person should make the case for why his or her example is more incredible than those that preceded it.

Then ask:

- Think back to times when you learned how something worked (such as a television or a computer or a telephone). Were you disappointed? Intrigued? Indifferent? Why?
- Would you say that you are content to be amazed by technology or natural phenomena, or are you curious and eager to uncover the whys and hows?
- When it comes to your faith, what piques your curiosity?

Opening Prayer

Lord, thank you for what we've learned during our time together, and give us wisdom and humility as we join together for this final session. Open our eyes to the ways you are at work among us and in the world around us. Open our ears to the ways you speak to us through one another, our stories, and our shared experiences. Bless this time we have together that we can learn from one another, from Scripture, and from your Holy Spirit. In Christ's name we pray. Amen.

WATCH DVD SEGMENT
(10 MINUTES)

STUDY AND DISCUSSION
(30–35 MINUTES)

<u>Note:</u> Discussion helps and questions that correspond to Chapter Four: "Bigger on the Inside" are provided below. If you have more time in your session, or want to include additional discussion and activities to your time, see "Additional Options for Bible Study and Discussion" at the end of this section, listed after the Closing Activity and Prayer.

1+1+1=1

(See *The Salvation of Doctor Who,* pages 97–100.)

For discussion:

- Can you think of any phenomena for which there are no known explanations? (If some of the examples listed have explanations, allow participants to offer them; just be careful not to spend too much time on this question.)
- How important it is to you to have an explanation for these phenomena?

Read aloud or summarize for the group:

Rawle's final chapter focuses on the TARDIS, the Doctor's time-traveling vehicle. The TARDIS appears on the outside to be a 1960s-era police box—a small booth or kiosk used in Great Britain as a miniature police station. But upon entering, passengers in the TARDIS discover that it is much larger than an ordinary police box. The dimensions on the inside of the TARDIS are much greater than those on the outside, a fact that is never fully explained. The particulars of how the TARDIS works remain an enigma even to the most devoted Whovians, but, as Rawle writes, "explaining interdimensional drafts just might be easier than understanding or explaining the Trinity."

For discussion:

- If someone with little or no knowledge of Christianity asked you, "What is the deal with the Trinity?" what would you say? (Assume that you don't have time to do any research or consult with your pastor.)
- What questions do you have about the Trinity?
- Rawle writes, "When the Doctor enters the scene, we see a blue box. When God enters our lives, we experience Father, Son, and Spirit." In what ways have you seen, or experienced, God entering the world?
- How have you experienced God in the person of Jesus Christ?
- How have you experienced God in the person of the Holy Spirit?
- Through what person of the Trinity have you experienced God most closely or clearly?

The Trinity in Scripture

Activity:

The Bible never actually uses the word *Trinity* to describe the three persons of God, but plenty of verses refer to the Father, Christ, and Holy Spirit, and the relationships between the three. Look at some or all of the following Scriptures. Discuss what each one says about the Trinity, the relationships between the persons of the Trinity, and/or why the Trinity is essential to the Christian faith.

- Matthew 3:13–17
- Matthew 28:18–20
- John 14:15–17
- 2 Corinthians 13:13
- Philippians 2:5–8

A more complete understanding of the Trinity developed over the first few centuries of Christianity. Read the portion of the Athanasian Creed that Rawle includes on page 94. This creed is named for Athanasius of Alexandria, a fourth-century bishop instrumental in articulating the relationships between the persons of the Trinity during the Council of Nicaea.

After reading this portion of the creed, ask:

- Which of your questions about the Trinity does this creed answer?
- Which new questions does it raise?
- How does this creed help you better understand the relationships between God the Father, Christ, and the Holy Spirit?

Bigger on the Inside

(See *The Salvation of Doctor Who,* pages 100–104.)

Read aloud or summarize for the group:

Those who are fortunate enough to enter the TARDIS soon discover that it is much more impressive than its facade suggests—that it is much bigger on the inside than its outer dimensions would seem to allow. Like the TARDIS, God is also bigger and more impressive than our first impressions would suggest.

For discussion:

- What was your first impression of the God of Christ? If you grew up in the church, what was the earliest impression of God you remember having? If you encountered the Christian faith later in life, how did you first understand the three-in-one God?
- How has your understanding of God grown and changed since then?
- In what ways has God gotten bigger, either in terms of how you understand who God is or in terms of how you understand what God is doing?

Note to the Leader: On a computer, tablet, phone, or other device bring up an image of Andrei Rublev's *Trinity* icon. (You might have individual participants pull up the icon on their phones.) Rublev painted the three strangers who visited Abraham in Genesis 18:1–15, but the painting historically has been interpreted as an icon of the Trinity. Give everyone a chance to look at the icon then ask:

- Why, do you think, has this painting been associated with the Trinity? What is it about the three figures that brings to mind the three persons of the Trinity?

Read aloud or summarize for the group:

Rawle writes,

> The most surprising thing about Rublev's icon painting is that there is actually a fourth person in the picture—you! This represents how God invites us into his own heart, giving us a place at the table. God invites us to actively participate in what he is doing in the world.... The Trinity is a picture of who God is—the Lover, the Beloved, and the love they share. The awesome thing is that when we share love with each other through kindness, generosity, and service, we share the very essence of God.

For discussion:

- What do you think Rawle means when he says that there is a fourth person in the picture? How are you in the picture?
- How is God, by God's very essence, a relationship? How is God "Lover, Beloved, and the love they share?"
- What are ways that we can and do participate in this love we see at work in the Trinity?
- Does this icon, or the idea that relationship is at the heart of who God is, further expand your understanding of God? If so, how?

Fish Fingers and Custard, in Remembrance of Me
(See *The Salvation of Doctor Who,* pages 113–15.)

Note to Leader: As you near the end of this study, celebrate by sharing refreshments. Though you are not participating in the sacrament of Holy Communion, the food and drink you share recalls the meal that Jesus shared with his disciples before his death, the meal in which he told his followers, "Do this in remembrance of me" (Luke 22:19).

For discussion:

Read Luke 22:14–20 aloud, and ask:

- What is Jesus telling us to do in remembrance of him? Is he simply telling us to have a meal, or is there something more?
- How can we, as the church, make sure that our celebrations of Holy Communion do what Jesus calls us to do in remembrance of him? How can they be about more than just bread and wine, or grape juice?
- What does Rawle mean when he says, " Holy Communion is like our own little time machine"? How does time become "wibbly-wobbly" at the Communion table?
- River Song, in *Doctor Who*, says, "Some days, everybody lives." What does this mean for Christians—that everybody lives? How does Holy Communion celebrate this life?

Closing Activity
(5 minutes)

Ask the group:

- What is one thing you learned from this session that you didn't know before? (Participants could name something they learned about Scripture; something they learned about one another; or even something interesting they learned about *Doctor Who*.)

- What is one important truth about God as the Trinity that you will take away from this session?
- What is one important truth about your identity as God's traveling companion that you will take away from this session?

If time permits:

Invite participants to imagine they can hop into the TARDIS and travel one week into the future. What would they like to have learned or accomplished during this coming week? Encourage participants to make a personal goal for themselves this week, perhaps using the SMART acronym as a guideline. (See page 19 in Session 1.)

Possible goals might include being intentional about welcoming any visitors they see during the next worship service (see "Always Alone But Never Alone") or finding a way to bring beauty to someone who is suffering ("Sunflowers").

Provide paper and pen for each person so participants can write down these goals as a reminder for the week. Some may want to share their goals with the group.

CLOSING PRAYER

Lord, thank you for this time we've had together over the past few weeks. Thank you for the witness of those in the past; thank you for the ways you've blessed us in the present; and thank you for the opportunities we have to grow and serve you in the future. Bless us as we go from here that we might participate in the work you call us to do, deliver your message of good news to all who need to hear it, and offer beauty and hope to those who are suffering. We pray all these things in Jesus' name. Amen.

ADDITIONAL OPTIONS FOR BIBLE STUDY AND DISCUSSION

Follow Me and Live Dangerously (10 minutes)

Activity:

Though it is a privilege and an honor to be chosen as one of the Doctor's traveling companions, it is also a dangerous gig that requires a great deal of trust and sacrifice. In other words, it's a lot like following Jesus.

Read Mark 1:16–20, in which Jesus calls his first disciples. Ask:

- Why, do you think, did Simon, Andrew, James, and John decide to follow Jesus?
- What did they give up when they decided to follow Jesus? What risks did they take?

As a group, brainstorm a list of "cons" of following Jesus. Identify the risks, drawbacks, and discomforts that go along with being a disciple of Christ. Focus specifically on the challenges that Christians face today in your part of the world. (For instance, Jesus' teachings on greed and wealth are often at odds with what culture values; showing compassion to strangers and those who are most vulnerable can expose us to danger.)

After you've put together a good list of reasons *not* to be a Christian, ask participants to make a convincing case for following Christ, despite all of the cons. Then ask:

- What do you think are the most compelling reasons for being a disciple of Jesus?

- How do you maintain a relationship with Christ amid the challenges, sacrifices, and dangers?

Always Alone but Never Alone (15–20 minutes)

(See *The Salvation of Doctor Who*, pages 104–7.)

Read aloud or summarize for the group:

It may seem ridiculous for the TARDIS to be so enormous on the inside until you consider that the Doctor often doesn't travel alone. Over the decades *Doctor Who* has been on the air, the Doctor has been joined by numerous traveling companions. The Doctor is a survivor of a great Time War, who assumed for centuries that he was the last of his kind. Rather than travel by himself and wallow in loneliness and bitterness, the Doctor finds people he finds interesting and asks them to accompany him.

For discussion:

- Think of some traveling companions whose company you've enjoyed (perhaps on a family vacation, a college road trip, or business travel). How did this person make your travels more enjoyable or fulfilling? How would the trip have been different without her or his company?
- Rawle connects this discussion of the Doctor's companions to the topic of evangelism. What comes to mind when you hear the word *evangelism*?
- What does *evangelism* actually mean? (*Evangelism* literally means to bring a message of good news. For Christians, *evangelism* means bringing the message of Christ to those who have not heard it, or who need to hear it again or in a new way.)

- Do you agree with Rawle that the word sometimes takes on negative connotations? Why, or why not?
- What is the relationship between evangelism and Rawle's discussion of the Doctor's traveling companions? (You might say that evangelism is inviting companions to join us on our journey.)

Activity:

Have participants pair off to discuss when they have heard God calling them. They might think back to their first encounter with Christ, or they might reflect on a time when God called them to take their lives in a particular direction. Allow pairs to discuss for a couple minutes. Then ask them to think and talk about ways that other people were involved in these experiences. How did God work through friends, family, acquaintances, and even strangers to bring them into a relationship or call them to a particular vocation?

Then have participants switch partners and talk about ways in which God has worked through them to draw people into a relationship with Christ and the church. If they struggle to think of ways that they have been evangelists, they should reflect on ways that God could use them to deliver the message of Christ.

After participants have had time to think about how they, as individuals, have acted as evangelists, consider how your congregation does evangelism. Divide a markerboard or large sheet of paper into two columns. Label one, "Do well," and the other, "Needs improvement." Brainstorm ways in which your church has been successful with evangelism and list these in the first column. This might include having friendly greeters to welcome visitors, serving the community through outreach programs, or showing people Christ's love by your example.

Then brainstorm ways that your church could improve its evangelism efforts. List these in the second column. Maybe you could do a better job inviting and welcoming those who live in your church's neighborhood; maybe you host events that bring in a lot of people but don't do much to introduce these people to Christ or invite them to be part of a Christian community.

As a group, select one way that you could take the initiative to improve your congregation's evangelism efforts. This may be as simple as making sure that every visitor to worship is welcomed and invited to attend Sunday school or participate in another ministry of the church. If your idea involves established ministries or programs or starting a new ministry or program, make sure to work through the appropriate committees and staff members.

Sunflowers (15 minutes)
(See *The Salvation of Doctor Who,* pages 108–12.)

Read Rawle's account of the "Vincent and the Doctor" episode, in which the Doctor and companion Amy Pond visit artist Vincent van Gogh.

For discussion:

- How did the Doctor and Amy add to the "good" in Vincent's life?
- Vincent still took his own life in a fit of depression. Does this mean that the Doctor and Amy's efforts were in vain? Why, or why not?
- Why, do you think, did Vincent decide to dedicate "Sunflowers" to Amy instead of another painting? What, do you think, was the significance of sunflowers?
- Read through Rawle's account of working on hurricane relief in New Orleans and meeting Ms. Helena, who saw

God at work in the flood that destroyed her home. When have you been in despair because of something far less devastating than a flood that destroyed your house?

- How have you glimpsed God at work in an otherwise unfortunate situation?
- Where, or in whom, do you find hope in the midst of despair? How do you keep from losing sight of this hope?

Read aloud or summarize for the group:

The biblical figure most known for suffering likely is Job, who loses his family, health, and property overnight. The Book of Job concludes with God answering Job's cries (in Job 38–42). Rawle suggests that God is taking Job on "a tour of the universe," showing him, "the most beautiful sights any single human has ever seen."

For discussion:

- How might God's response to Job have brought hope to his suffering?
- In what ways do we today surround people with beauty, giving them hope amid despair?
- Romans 5:3–5, says, "We even take pride in our problems, because we know that trouble produces endurance, endurance produces character, and character produces hope. This hope doesn't put us to shame, because the love of God has been poured out in our hearts through the Holy Spirit, who has been given to us." What steps does Paul, the author of these verses, name as part of the process from suffering to hope? How, in your experience, does one step lead to the next?
- How can we guide and assist those who are making the journey from suffering to hope?

NOTE

Session 2: God and Time and God's Time

1. "The Satan Pit," *Doctor Who* (series 2, episode 9), British Broadcasting Corporation One (London: BBC, June 10, 2006).

CPSIA information can be obtained at www.ICGtesting.com
Printed in the USA
LVOW07s2148080815

449285LV00004B/5/P